Thoughts

Jennifer York

Presentation by *BookLeaf Publishing*

Web: www.bookleafpub.com

E-mail: info@bookleafpub.com

ISBN: 9789357618052

First edition 2022

Dedicated to you.

PREFACE

Emotions run wild in these first set of poems. From despair and loneliness to having my cup run over with blessings. I hope you enjoy and maybe even relate to some moments in these pages.

Thoughts

There is no time to ponder new deeply felt
emotions,
or how to absorb them to be put into motion.

There is no ability to stop day speeding into
night,
just hanging a hat on wonder-thoughts of maybe
and just might.

Euphonious timbres of friendliness are stamped
upon the mind,
Rehearsed words are practiced then rhythmically
timed.

Not knowing when motion of kindness will echo
once more,
reminiscent of powerful waves hugging the
shore.

Freedom

Freedom means more now, being grown with
children of my own.
Safety of knowing we are allowed to be different
than what our ancestors have shown.

Education, matrimony and enjoying the arts, are
all trusted and put in our hands.
Left to explore our big hearts, unique brains and
vast lands.

Let the amber waves of grain show the splendor
of the earth.
How a simple strand of wheat can be a sign of
rebirth.

Never take for granted what we have been given,
say thanks everyday.
You never know if and when our freedom could
be taken away.

Everything Will Be Alright

My heart goes out to you my Son, who is not
feeling up to par.
Your brow is dripping hot with sweat and your
lungs pull air like tar.
I will check on you tonight my dear, each time
that I awake.
I know it will happen often too- because your
pain I can not shake.
You are growing up so fast young boy- I hope
you know I care.
Hugs and kisses, squeezes and coos- I am your
Momma Bear.
My sleep will not come easy- with worry it will
be a long night.
You will be better soon my love and everything
will be alright.

Haiku

Hands slide in pockets.
Eyes gaze down to the ground.
Sadness takes over.

Gaze

5

The lure of your gaze causes adrenaline lustered
cheeks,
Directed eyes turn away.

The whisper of your gaze demands to listen
deeply,
Judgement not conveyed.

The embrace of your gaze broadens breathing,
Brown iris's deep in thought.

The caress of your gaze accelerates pulse,
Eyes lock serendipitously.

The devotion of your gaze fills vacancies,
A hint of promise welcomed.

Lure to embrace. Caress with whispers. Forever
promise. Gaze.

Quiet

A space sacred to my being.
A freedom from the incessant noise.

Just the voices in my head.

Give me the space, the place and freedom which
I so desire.

Shhhhh I just need quiet.

Speak

Never have I fallen so deeply into someone
because of their voices timbre.
The tender sounds calm my mind and stops the
meaningless meander.

Your steadfast voice is intoxicating, enfolding
me in an embrace.
It's not your body, build or frame, not even your
perfect face.

I could sit for hours and listen to your tranquil
flawless speech. I would right now if you were
not so far and out of reach.

Instead I will wish to dream, with your call
narrating the tale. Waking warm, blushed and
quivering, releasing a much needed exhale.

Affection

What is affection but to distract from the
mundane,
the pause in the day that takes your breath away.

What is affection but to preoccupy the mind,
the thoughts that consume every moment.

What is affection but to tantalize the body,
the fleeting glance soaring across the room.

What is affection but to dream of contentment,
the amiable feeling of asylum.

What is affection but to desire and be desired,
the merger of being as one.

What is affection but to love.

My Son

My Son you are turning into a well adjusted
man.
I've been watching firsthand as your Mother and
your number one fan.

Cubby babyface cheeks that would cuddle, turn
away from my kisses and land on stubble.

The door to your room is often found shut, but
not the door to your heart.
Treating people with kindness, even when it's
not cool is what you example from the start.

Eyes rolling in protest every once in awhile, can
change into rare hugs that come with a smile.

The next few years will be a rollercoaster of
emotions testing you this way and that.

You are strong and confidant and can do lots of
things, but do not have nine lives like the cat.

And as you turn further from teen into man,
remember my Son, I will always be your Mother
and number one fan.

Jealousy

The stinging pangs of envy reached its mark
today,
After flailing around and showing off for its
backbiting twin, jealousy.

The crushing emotion of defeat weighs heavy on
the heart, wanting something that is not
obtainable, wanting someone who is not
obtainable.

The relentless pining becomes complacent.
This is much more.
Unyielding passion is eating its victim alive.
Obsession.

Never out of mind.
Never forgotten.
Always wanting.
Always wondering.

The devastating realization of knowing that this
will never be is near impossible to accept. The
though of it is euphoric, the reality would be
detrimental. Upheaval of lives is not worth the

chance. To wait is the only thing that makes sense.

Waiting is not easy.

Dream

I feel safe when I am around you. I know you will listen to my side. I am not afraid of looking foolish, or damaging my pride.

I feel warm when I'm beside you. I know you will have my back. I'm not afraid to divulge to you, my not so innocent track.

I feel invited when I'm with you. I know I will not be an outsider. I'm not afraid to reach out to you, and share my deep desires.

I feel cheated when we're apart. I know it won't last long. I'm not afraid to to pine for you, and tell you together we belong.

I feel betrayed with the realizing the truth of this facade. I know we are not supposed to be a team. I know to be apart of your strong loving kindness, I can only dream.

Alone

Someday the rain will come and wash away my
tears.
The tears that drape down my cheeks and show
all my fears.

Fears of waking up one morning in an empty,
lonely house.
Memories of being abandoned on a doorstep
dressed in a tattered blouse.

The blouse that wrapped me and kept me warm
was from a young scared mother.
Who could not take care for her young baby so
gave her to two others.

The others raised me, loved me well and
supported my every dream.
I could not have asked to be apart of a better
family team.

The team is mine forever, no-one can take that
away.
But someday the team will have to disband and
to heaven they will astray.

My fears of utter aloneness is always on my
mind.
But some day the rain will come and a rainbow
will then shine.

A.L.O.N.E.

15

Always am I falling in love, with people that do not return the gesture.

Leaving me with my thoughts, that I am not enough.

Others say they see me, love to be around me, but don't take the time to look into my mind.

Not once being first priority, proclaiming I'm the one. Not one single person wanting me more than anyone else. No one.

Enough of this need of belonging , I will live with my mind alone. Being complacent with myself should keep my mind at ease.

Banana Bread

Banana bread oh banana bread, I love you
banana bread.
Breakfast? Banana bread.
Snack? Banana bread.
Dessert? Banana bread.
Share it or not you can never go wrong as long
as you bring banana bread along.
Picnics and brunch- potlucks or lunch.
Banana bread you are so sweet.
Banana bread you can not be beat.

The Dreamer

Gentle are your eyes as is your clam demeanor.
The way you wrap me with your voice makes
me a hopeless dreamer.

I want nothing but to sit with you and talk the
day away. Speaking feelings and dreams and
silly things that remind me of play.

Anxious is my mind because I know we can not
be. I know because that would ruin two good
wholesome families.

It's not your body that I so crave. Not your
hands nor build nor stature. It's your deep
beautiful mind that entangles me in rapture.

I shall stay alone in my thoughts of what-ifs and
my why-nots. Of who would have done that and
this and all those what-nots.

It's not that I'm unhappy in my exclusive marital
arrangement. It's that I don't think he knew there
is more than just saying you're in a commitment.

To nurture each other for years upon years, is
supposed to be full of smiles not tears.

I wish he knew how I need him to support. To
listen and be present and tell me he loves me. To
hold my hand and lean upon me and be a
partnership for eternity.

I hate feeling alone and used only for his wishes.
I want him to help me be strong and ambitious.

I want him to wrap me with a gentle calm
demeanor. Be the one that listens deeply. The
one that I can talk to and look at and make me
feel so dreamy.

Haiku-Bedtime

19

Blanket pulled to chin
Arms wrap tightly around me
Sleep turns to slumber

I Feel

I feel safe when I am around you. I know you will listen to my side. I am not afraid of looking foolish, or damaging my pride.

I feel warm when I'm beside you. I know you will have my back. I'm not afraid to divulge to you, my not so innocent track.

I feel invited when I'm with you. I know I will not be an outsider. I'm not afraid to reach out to you, and share my deep desires.

I feel cheated when we're apart. I know it won't be long. I'm not afraid to to pine for you, and tell you we belong.

I feel betrayed with the realizing this is a foolish facade. I know we are not a team. I am afraid that to be apart of your love, it can only be in a dream.

Eyes II

Eyes II
Your eyes are alluring , pulling me in like a hug.
I can't break away from them, they hypnotize
like a drug.

You seem to feel the pull into each other as well
as I do.
That long pause when eyes lock, who looks
away first? Who?

This gaze pierces right into my beating lonely
heart.
I can't think of anything else but it, when we are
apart.

How do eyes have power to control, at the same
time soothe?
For just three seconds my body can't move.

Thinking of them still, I need to pause and
breathe.
Only then calmness takes over and I pray you
don't leave.

Keep me here in your embrace to look deeply
into those eyes.
They are holding me captive, fascinated, deeply
mesmerized.

www.ingramcontent.com/pod-product-compliance
Lightning Source LLC
LaVergne TN
LVHW050506210726
843509LV00015BA/3020